This book is designed to provide information and guidance in regard to the subject matter concerned. It is to be used as a study guide for preparing for classroom exams and certification exams. It is not meant to be a clinical manual. The reader is advised to consult textbooks and other reference manuals in making clinical decisions. It is not the purpose of this book to reprint all the information that is otherwise available, but rather to assist the student in organizing the material to facilitate study and recall on exams. Although every precaution has been taken in the preparation of this book, the publisher, author, and members of the editorial board assume no responsibility for errors, omissions or typographical mistakes. Nor is any liability assumed for damages resulting from the direct and indirect use of the information contained herein. To the best of our knowledge, the book contains information that is up-to-date up to the printing date. Due to the very nature of the medical profession, there will be points out-of-date as soon as the book is available to you. If you do not wish to be bound by the above, you may return this book for a full refund if a monetary cost was incurred in obtaining the book.

Rosh RAPID REVIEW

for the PANCE / PANRE

1st Edition

Endocrine System

Yehuda Wolf, PA-C

Emily Oslie, PA-C

Adam Rosh, MD

Your Content Creation Team

Yehuda Wolf, PA-C

Yehuda joined the Rosh team in 2015 while still a student in PA school. As Rapid Review author and editor-in-chief, Yehuda continues to ensure the Rapid Reviews are of the highest caliber and standards. Yehuda graduated from Touro College New York with a Masters in Physician Assistant Studies with Honors. Yehuda currently spends his time between a busy pediatric primary care practice and pediatric surgical urology.

Emily Oslie, PA-C

Emily Oslie graduated with a B.S. in applied human biology from Seattle Pacific University where she played volleyball competitively. After graduation, she worked as a medical scribe in emergency departments and a primary care office in Seattle while applying to PA programs. Emily attended the Duke Physician Assistant Program where she served as class president and earned her PA certification and masters in health sciences. She is currently working at Duke Urgent Care in Durham, North Carolina.

Adam Rosh, MD

Dr. Adam Rosh is the founder of Rosh Review, which he created in 2011. He received his B.A. in biochemistry and M.S. in microbiology from the University of Wisconsin, Madison. He received his medical degree from Rutgers Medical School and completed his emergency medicine residency training at New York University/Bellevue Hospital Center, where he was chief resident. Dr. Rosh went on to serve as assistant residency director and residency director at Detroit Receiving Hospital. He is the author and editor of Pretest Emergency Medicine and Case Files Emergency Medicine both published by McGraw Hill. He currently is the CEO of Rosh Review and an Attending Emergency Physician.

Your Content Support Team

Kristian Savic, Copy Editor

Kristian is Senior Content Editor at Rosh Review. Originally hailing from Salzburg, Austria, his training includes three years in med school, a B.S. in communication sciences, and an M.A. in German literature—all of which helped in creating the passionate stickler for format, grammar, and bio-science terminology he is today. Kristian's work is focused on making sure Rosh Review content is well written, correct, and adhering to our house style and good science writing standards.

Erica Parrish, Content Manager

Erica Parrish received her B.A. in biology from the College of St. Scholastica and her D.C. from Northwestern Health Sciences University. She gained clinical experience serving patients in both Minnesota and Florida before joining the team at Rosh Review.

All Of You, Content Impactors

Although most of the content in this book was created by our author team, over the years we've received so much input from our subscribers, we want to shine a light on this contribution. Every comment or feedback email we receive is reviewed, discussed, and if agreed upon, implemented. The power of all of you, contributing your experience and insights, allows us to continually improve the quality of the content we publish. This process is perpetual. As medicine changes, our content must change with it. We value the content partnership we have and hope you'll continue to raise expectations.

Shout Outs

Yehuda Wolf, PA-C

I am still in shell shock. This project has been years in the making and the original reason why I ever reached out to Adam. I can't believe we are finally done. First, I need to thank my most amazing wife and children for their unparalleled support and encouragement. Thank you for allowing me to do work after I finally got home from work. A special thank you to my mentors Dr. Hylton Lightman, MD and Dov Landa, PA-C whose mentorship and guidance continually make me a better provider to my patients. Thanks to my right-hand Emily and the rest of the team, Kristian and Erica. You are truly the ink to my pen, the paper to my pad and without you this project would be nothing but a sloppy mess in my mind. Thank you Adam for your constant support and encouragement. Always pushing us "one step further." Finally, I would like to thank the One Above for His Goodness and His Grace that He has shown me throughout my life. May this be the first of many more projects to come. In the words of the ancient physician Maimonides, "Never allow the thought to arise in me that I have attained to sufficient knowledge, but vouchsafe to me the strength, the leisure and the ambition ever to extend my knowledge. For art is great, but the mind of man is ever expanding."

Emily Oslie, PA-C

This is is for my parents, Myron and Sherri, who have cheered me on through each phase of my education and career; my sister, Maddie; my classmates at Duke who supported me and are the reason I have countless fond memories of my time in the program; the instructors, advisors, and clinical preceptors who challenged me to become a compassionate and competent provider; my co-providers, mentor, supervising physician, and patients at Duke Urgent Care who make me a better PA every day.

Adam Rosh, MD

A hearty thanks goes out to my family for their love and support, Danielle, Ruby, Rhys, and especially my parents, Karl and Marcia; the incredibly dedicated team at Rosh Review who relentlessly raise expectations; the committed medical professionals of Rutgers Medical School, the emergency medicine departments at New York University/Bellevue Hospital Center, and Wayne State University/Detroit Receiving Hospital; and my patients, who put their trust in me, and teach me something new each day.

Purpose & Goals
of this Book

Learning and education is a dynamic process, one that is never ending. Once we commit to a life in medicine, we commit to a life of learning. The Rosh Rapid Review book series is best suited to serve as an adjunct to your medical education. It is not meant as a primary source, rather it should help you organize your thoughts and provide ancillary knowledge for a more robust education. We are counting on you to not just regurgitate facts, but rather, paraphrasing Dr. Elizabeth Blackburn, to learn how it all works. We are privileged to be in the role of caretaker and thus have a responsibility to our patients to be the most knowledgeable we can be. Use this book on your learning journey. At some point, you will grow out of it. But in the meantime, we hope the hard work by the dedicated Rosh Review team can play just a small role in helping you reach your goals and achieve your dreams.

Adam Rosh, MD
Founder, Rosh Review

"To study the phenomena of disease without books is to sail an uncharted sea, while to study books without patients is not to go to sea at all."

William Osler, Aequanimatas

"I didn't want to just know the names of things. I remember really wanting to know how it all worked."

Elizabeth Blackburn,
Nobel Prize for Physiology or Medicine

Rosh ✓ Core Values

1. We pay attention to detail and always deliver the highest quality content.

2. We believe it is a privilege to interact with and care for individuals.

3. We are always learning and continuously self improving, it is part of our DNA.

Even after multiple reviews, there is sure to be mistakes in this book. As part of Rosh Review's culture of continuously learning, please let us know if you identify an error by sending us an email to alwaysimproving@roshreview.com

Let's get started...

Endocrine System

Table of Contents

|

I. Adrenal Disorders

PRIMARY ADRENAL INSUFFICIENCY • CUSHING SYNDROME

A. Primary Adrenal Insufficiency (Addison's Disease)

Pathophysiology
- **Most common** cause is **autoimmune**

Presentation
- Abdominal pain, nausea, vomiting, diarrhea, fever, and confusion

Physical Exam
- **Hyperpigmentation** of the skin and mucous membranes

Diagnostic Studies
- Hypotension
- **Hypo**natremia, **hyper**kalemia, hypoglycemia

↓ sugar Na⁺   ↑ K⁺

Management
- **Hydrocortisone**

Primary ⤳ *hypothalamic pituitary adrenal*   *↓ cortisol ↑ ACTH*
- HPA axis is intact
- Decreased cortisol release
- Increased ACTH levels (due to negative feedback)
- Most commonly from autoimmune destruction of adrenal cortex

Secondary   *↓ ACTH ↓ cortisol*
- HPA axis *not* intact
- Lack of ACTH
- Impaired stimulation of adrenal glands

Hypothalamus

Corticotrophin releasing hormone (CRH)

Pituitary gland

Adrenocorticotropic hormone (ACTH) & Melanocyte stimulating hormone (MSH)

Adrenal gland

Cortisol

3   Low cortisol leads to increased CRH release via **negative feedback** loop

2   Increased CRH leads to increased ACTH and increased MSH (hyperpigmentation)

1   **Destruction of adrenal cortex** leads to decreased cortisol release which results in lack of **negative feedback** to hypothalamus

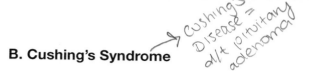

B. Cushing's Syndrome

Pathophysiology

- **Most commonly** caused by **exogenous steroids** or **hypercortisolism** from **ACTH-secreting pituitary tumor**

Presentation

- Amenorrhea, **central obesity**, depressive symptoms, easy bruising

Physical Exam

- **Purple striae**, **"moon facies"** (facial adiposity), **"buffalo hump"** (increased adipose tissue in the neck and upper back), and **hypertension**

Diagnostic Studies

- **24-hour urine cortisol**
- Serum ACTH

Comments

- If caused by pituitary tumor, the condition is termed **Cushing's Disease**

Due to **excess cortisol-like medication** (prednisone) or tumor that produces or results in production of **excessive cortisol [Cases due to pituitary adenoma = Cushing's disease]**

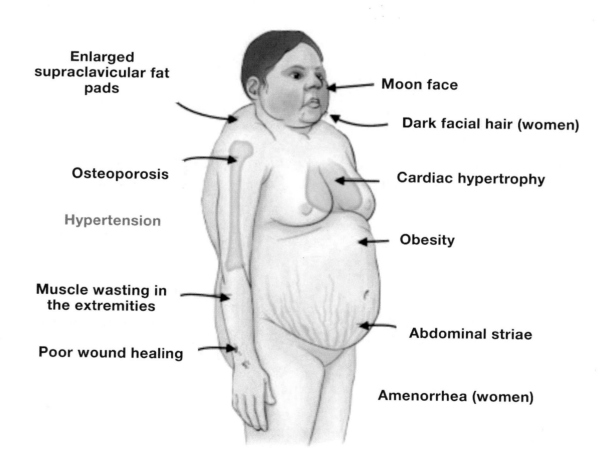

II. Diabetes Mellitus

TYPE 1 • TYPE 2

autoimmune

A. Diabetes Mellitus: Type 1 → *autoimmune*

Pathophysiology
- **Most commonly** caused by **autoimmune destruction of pancreatic beta cells**

Patient
- Child

Presentation
- **Polydipsia, polyphagia, polyuria, weight loss**

Diagnostic Studies
- **ADA Diagnostic Criteria**
- Symptoms plus one of the following:
  - **Random** plasma glucose of **> 200 mg/dL**
  - **Fasting** plasma glucose of **> 126 mg/dL** on **two** separate occasions
  - Glycated hemoglobin (A1c) of **> 6.5 %**
  - Plasma glucose of **> 200 mg/dL two hours** after a **75 g glucose load** during an oral glucose tolerance test

Management
- **Insulin**

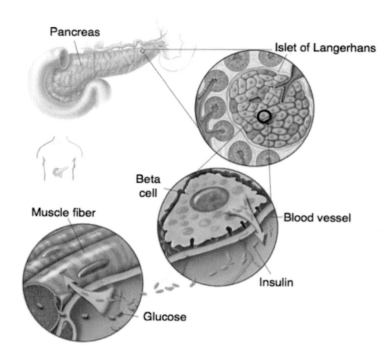

Pancreas
Islet of Langerhans
Beta cell
Muscle fiber
Blood vessel
Insulin
Glucose

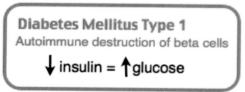

Diabetes Mellitus Type 1
Autoimmune destruction of beta cells

↓ insulin = ↑ glucose

B. Diabetes Mellitus Type 2 → *insulin resistant*

Pathophysiology
- **Most commonly** caused by **insulin resistance**

Patient
- Middle-aged, **obese**

Presentation

- **Polydipsia**, **polyphagia**, **polyuria**

Diagnostic Studies (same as DM 1)

- **ADA Diagnostic Criteria**
- Symptoms plus one of the following:
  - **Random** plasma glucose of **> 200 mg/dL**
  - **Fasting** plasma glucose of **> 126 mg/dL** on **two** separate occasions
  - Glycated hemoglobin (A1c) of **> 6.5 %**
  - Plasma glucose of **> 200 mg/dL two hours** after a **75 g glucose load** during an oral glucose tolerance test

Management

- Lifestyle modifications, then medication (**Metformin** is first-line)

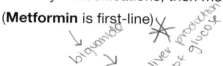

biguanide
↓ liver production of glucose

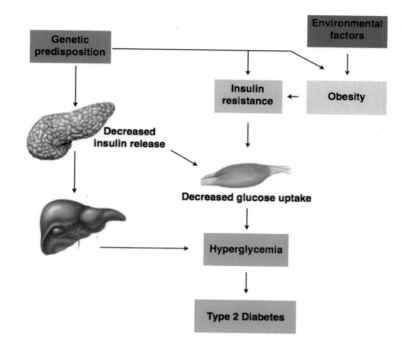

Diabetes Type 2 Medication Classes			
Class	**Common Drugs**	**Mechanism**	**Hypoglycemia**
Biguanides	Metformin	Decreases hepatic gluconeogenesis	No
Sulfonylureas	Glyburide, Glipizide	Increases insulin secretion	Yes
Thiazolidinediones	Pioglitazone, Rosiglitazone	Increases insulin sensitivity in muscle and fat	No
Meglitinides	Repaglinide, Nateglinide	Increases insulin secretion	Yes
α-glucosidase inhibitors	Acarbose, Miglitol	Decreases intestinal absorption of carbohydrates	No
DPP-4 inhibitors	Sitagliptin, Saxagliptin	Increases insulin secretion	No
Glucagon-like peptide-1 agonists	Exenatide, Lixisenatide, Liraglutide, Dulaglutide	Increases insulin secretion and decreases glucagon secretion	No
Insulin	Regular, Lispro, Aspart, NPH, Glargine	Increases glucose uptake	Yes
Gliflozins Sodium/glucose cotransporter 2 (SGLT2) inhibitors	Dapagliflozin, Canagliflozin, Empagliflozin	Reduces reabsorption of filtered glucose in the proximal renal tubules resulting in increased urinary excretion of glucose and reducing plasma glucose	No

III. Hypogonadism

A. Hypogonadism

Presentation

- Sexual dysfunction, erectile dysfunction, decreased libido, fatigue, and decreased muscle mass

Diagnostic Studies

- **Primary** disorder (due to testicular malfunction)
  - FSH and LH **high** or high-normal
- **Secondary** disorder (due to a hypothalamic or pituitary cause)
  - FSH and LH **low** or low-normal

Comments

- Risk factors of acquired hypogonadism are opiate use, sleep apnea, and marijuana

Handwritten annotations:
- RF: opioid/drug/weed use, sleep apnea
- ↓ testosterone
- ↑ FSH & LH → i.e. Turner or Kleinfelter
- ↓ FSH & LH, ↓ testosterone
- i.e. Kallmann syndrome
- all hypothalamic or pituitary prob

PRIMARY Hypogonadism
Testicular dysfunction
(Defect lies within the gonad)

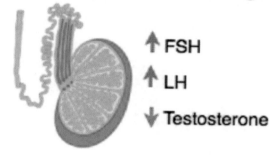

↑ FSH

↑ LH

↓ Testosterone

- Klinefelter syndrome
- Turner syndrome

SECONDARY Hypogonadism
Pituitary or Hypothalamic dysfunction
(Defect lies outside the gonad)

↓ FSH

↓ LH

↓ Testosterone

- Kallmann syndrome

IV. Neoplasms

MULTIPLE ENDOCRINE NEOPLASIA • NEOPLASTIC SYNDROME • PRIMARY ENDOCRINE MALIGNANCY
SYNDROME OF INAPPROPRIATE ANTIDIURETIC HORMONE SECRETION (SIADH)

A. Multiple Endocrine Neoplasia (MEN)

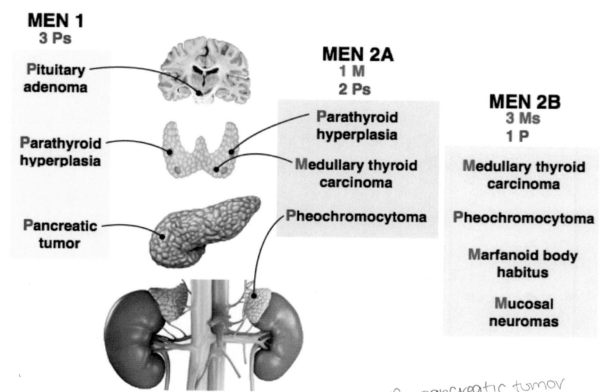

1 → pituitary adenoma, parathyroid hyperplasia, pancreatic tumor

2a → parathyroid hyperplasia, pheochromocytoma, medullary thyroid carcinoma

2b → pheochromocytoma, medullary thyroid carcinoma, marfanoid body habitus, mucosal neuromas

B. Pheochromocytoma

Pathophysiology
- **Most commonly** caused by a **catecholamine-secreting tumor** located in the **adrenal glands**

Presentation
- **Headaches, flushing, tremors,** and **vision changes**

Physical Exam
- Hypertension

Diagnostic Studies
- Assay of **urinary catecholamines** and **metanephrines,** and **plasma metanephrine levels**

Management
- Surgery; treat with **alpha-blocker** (phenoxybenzamine) prior to beta-blockade to prevent unopposed alpha agonism

Diagnosis
- **Fractioned metanephrines** and **catecholamines** in 24-hour urine collection
- Plasma fractionated metanephrines
- Normetanephrine, norepinephrine

Treatment
- Surgical resection of tumor
- Phenoxybenzamine (preop)
- Phentolamine (acute hypertensive crisis)
- Sodium nitroprusside (acute hypertensive crisis)
- Nicardipine (acute hypertensive crisis)

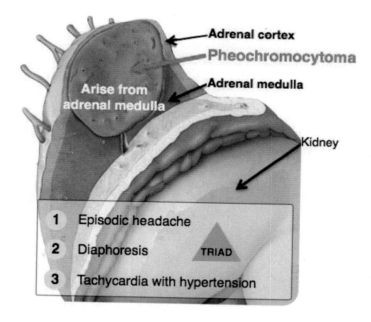

C. Primary Aldosteronism (Conn Syndrome)

Pathophysiology
- **Most commonly** caused by an aldosterone-**producing adrenal adenoma**

Physical Exam
- **Hypertension**

Diagnostic Studies
- Metabolic alkalosis, **hypernatremia**, unexplained **hypokalemia**

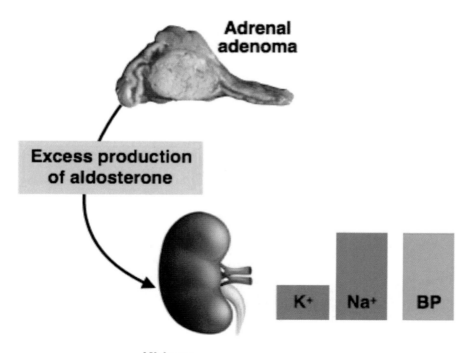

Kidney
- Sodium retention
- Water retention
- Increased intravascular volume
- Potassium loss
- Metabolic alkalosis

D. Syndrome of Inappropriate Antidiuretic Hormone Secretion (SIADH)

- Euvolemic hyponatremia that results from **persistent ADH** release **independent of serum osmolality**

<u>Diagnostic Studies</u>
- Labs will show a urine osmolality > 50 – 100 mOsm/kg in the setting of serum hypo-osmolarity without a physiologic reason for **increased** ADH (Ex: CHF, cirrhosis, hypovolemia)
- Urinary sodium level is often ≥ 40 mEq/L

<u>Management</u>
- Restrict fluid and address the underlying cause
- If hyponatremia is severe (< 110 mEq/L) or if the patient is significantly symptomatic (Ex: comatose, seizing), cautiously give hypertonic saline
  - Patients must be monitored in the ICU to prevent **central pontine myelinolysis**
- Demeclocycline, an **ADH receptor antagonist**, or **vasopressin receptor antagonists** (conivaptan) can help normalize serum sodium

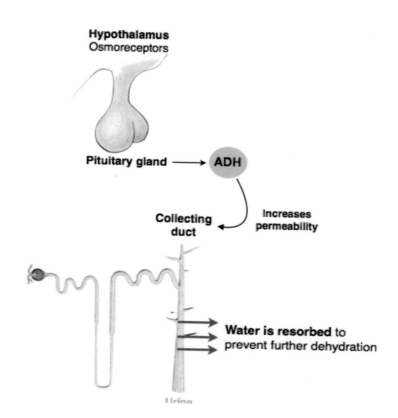

	Serum Na$^+$	Serum OSM	Urine OSM
SIADH	↓	↓	↑
Dehydration	↑	↑	↑
Diabetes insipidus	↑	↑	↓

V. Parathyroid Disorders

HYPERPARATHYROIDISM • HYPOPARATHYROIDISM

A. Hyperparathyroidism

Pathophysiology
- **Most commonly** caused by an **adenoma** with unregulated **overproduction** of PTH

Diagnostic Studies
- **High** PTH, **high** calcium, **low** phosphorus

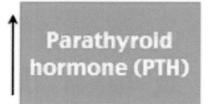
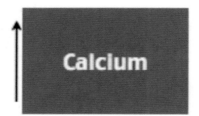

B. Hypoparathyroidism

<u>Patient</u>
- History of recent **thyroid** surgery

<u>Presentation</u>
- Extremity and **perioral paresthesias, tetany**, and lethargy

<u>Physical Exam</u>
- **Chvostek sign** (contraction of facial muscles with resultant twitching after tapping facial nerve)
- **Trousseau sign** (induction of carpopedal spasm)

<u>Diagnostic Studies</u>
- **Low** PTH, **low** calcium, **high** phosphorus

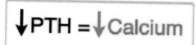

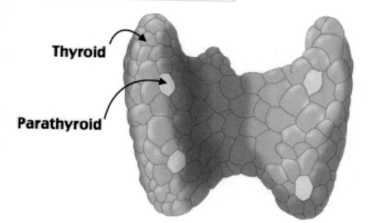

Causes
- Thyroid surgery
- Parathyroid surgery
- Autoimmune
- Infiltrative
- Familial
- Idiopathic

Hypocalcemia
- Tetany
- Chvostek sign (Contraction of facial muscles after tapping facial nerve)
- Trousseau sign (Induction of carpal pedal spasm)
- Paresthesias (Fingertips/perioral)
- Prolonged QT interval

VI. Pituitary Disorders

ACROMEGALY/GIGANTISM • DIABETES INSIPIDUS • DWARFISM • PITUITARY ADENOMA

A. Acromegaly

Pathophysiology
- **Most commonly** caused by **a pituitary adenoma**

Presentation
- **Increased** hat, glove, or shoe size

Physical Exam
- **Coarse facial features, oily skin, visual field deficits, diabetes**

Diagnostic Studies
- Labs will show increased **insulin-like growth factor**

Management
- **Transsphenoidal** resection

Enlargement of hands and feet

PITUITARY ADENOMA
Growth hormone excess

Weight gain

Glucose intolerance

Bone growth

Hypertension & hypertrophy

B. Diabetes Insipidus (DI)

Presentation
- **Polyuria, polydipsia**

Diagnostic Studies
- **Increase** in plasma osmolality and a **decrease** urine osmolality

Central DI

Pathophysiology
- **Most commonly** caused by **decrease ADH production**

Diagnostic Studies
- Water deprivation test: **> 50% increase** in **urine osmolality**

Management
- Intranasal **DDAVP**

Nephrogenic DI

Pathophysiology
- Caused by **renal unresponsiveness** to ADH

Patient
- **Lithium** use

Diagnostic Studies
- Water deprivation test: **no change** in **urine osmolality**

Management
- HCTZ, amiloride, indomethacin

|

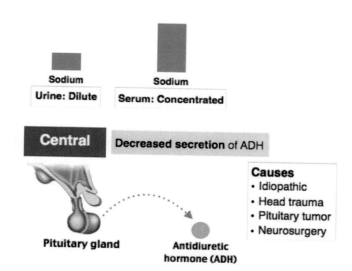

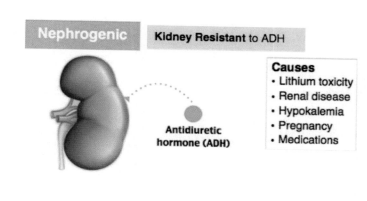

C. Pituitary Adenoma

<u>Pathophysiology</u>

- **Most common** tumors are **microadenomas** (< 10 mm) that are functional (hypersecretion of pituitary hormones)
  - **Prolactinoma**: Secretes prolactin causing **galactorrhea**, infertility, amenorrhea
  - **Non-Secreting Adenoma**: Null cell, no secretion
  - **Somatotroph Adenoma**: Growth hormone and prolactin secreting; presents as acromegaly
  - **Corticotroph Adenoma**: Increased ACTH leads to Cushing's Syndrome
  - **Thyrotroph Adenoma**: Increased TSH leads to **hyper**thyroidism

<u>Diagnostic Studies</u>

- **MRI** is the study of choice to look for **sellar** lesions or tumors
- Endocrine studies: prolactin, GH, ACTH, TSH, FSH, LH

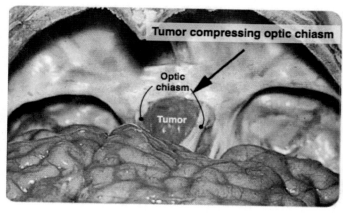

Bitemporal Hemianopsia

Loss of temporal field vison

Other Neurologic Findings
- Headache (expansion of sella)
- Diplopia (oculomotor nerve compression)
- Pituitary apoplexy (induced by hemorrhage)
- Infiltrative
- CSF rhinorrhea
- Parinaud syndrome

VII. Thyroid Disorders

HYPERTHYROIDISM • HYPOTHYROIDISM • THYROIDITIS

A. Hyperthyroidism

Pathophysiology
- **Most commonly** caused by **Graves' disease** (autoimmune, against TSH receptors)

Presentation
- **Heat intolerance**, **palpitations**, weight loss, and anxiety

Physical Exam
- **Tachycardia**, hyperreflexia, **goiter**, **exophthalmos**, pretibial edema

Diagnostic Studies
- **Low** TSH and **high** free T4

Management
- **Methimazole** or PTU

Comments
- **PTU if Pregnant**

B. Grave's Disease

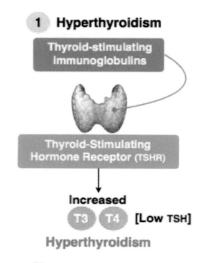

1 **Hyperthyroidism**

Thyroid-stimulating immunoglobulins

Thyroid-Stimulating Hormone Receptor (TSHR)

Increased
T3 T4 **[Low TSH]**

Hyperthyroidism

2 **Goiter**

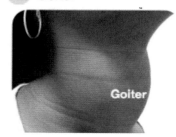

Goiter

3 **Eye disease**

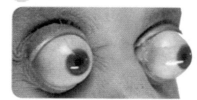

Exophthalmos
Abnormal connective tissue deposition

4 **Pretibial or localized edema**

An infiltrative dermopathy with waxy, discolored induration of the skin

C. Hypothyroidism

Pathophysiology
- **Most commonly** caused by **Hashimoto's thyroiditis**

Presentation
- Generalized weakness, **fatigue**, facial swelling, constipation, cold intolerance, weight gain

Physical Exam
- **Periorbital edema**, **dry skin**, and **coarse brittle hair**

Diagnostic Studies
- **High** TSH and **low** free T4, **antithyroid peroxidase**, and **antithyroglobulin** autoantibodies

Management
- Levothyroxine

Comments
- Monitor TSH serially; takes six weeks to see effect
- **Hashimoto's** is a risk factor for non-Hodgkin lymphoma

D. Hashimoto Thyroiditis

Chronic autoimmune thyroiditis

Most common cause of hypothyroidism in iodine-sufficient areas of the world

May present initially as **hyperthyroidism**

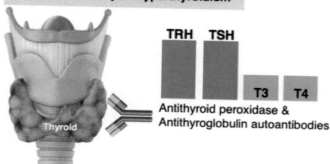

TRH   TSH

T3   T4

Antithyroid peroxidase & Antithyroglobulin autoantibodies

Thyroid

Clinical
- Fatigue
- Weight gain
- Cold intolerance
- Dry skin
- Constipation
- Menstrual irregularities
- Depression

Treatment
- Levothyroxine

E. Thyroid Function Test

Thyroid Function Test Interpretation			
TSH	Free T4	Free T3	Condition
Normal	Normal	Normal	• None
Low	High	High	• **Hyperthyroidism**
Low	Normal	Normal	• Subclinical hyperthyroidism
Low	Normal	High	• T3 toxicosis
Low	High	Normal	• Thyroiditis • T4 ingestion • Hyperthyroidism in the elderly or with comorbid illness
Low	Low	Low	• Euthyroid sick syndrome • Central hypothyroidism
High	Normal	Normal	• Subclinical hypothyroidism • Recovery from euthyroid sick syndrome
High	Low	Low	• **Primary hypothyroidism**
High	High	High	• TSH producing pituitary adenoma

F. Thyroid Carcinoma

Thyroid Carcinoma				
Type	Papillary	Follicular	Medullary	Anaplastic
Proportion of thyroid cancer	85%	12%	2%	1%
Age of incidence	35–40 yrs	30–60 yrs	Isolated: 40–50 yrs Genetic: 10–20 yrs	> 60 yrs
Cell differentiation	Well differentiated	Well differentiated	Intermediately differentiated	Poorly differentiated
Primary mode of spread	Lymphatic	Hematologic	Lymphatic	Lymphatic
Symptoms	Hoarseness Lymphadenopathy	Hoarseness Lymphadenopathy (rare)	Diarrhea Flushing	Shortness of breath Hoarseness Lymphadenopathy
Diagnosis	FNA	FNA and CNB to confirm	Fam history Previous MEN dx FNA Calcitonin level	CNB Surgical biopsy
Treatment	Surgery Radioablation TSH suppression	Surgery Radioablation TSH suppression	Surgery External beam radiation	Early: Surgery Late: Palliation
Prognosis	Excellent	Very good	Very good	Poor

FNA: Fine needle aspiration
CNB: Coarse needle biopsy
MEN: Multiple endocrine neoplasia

20 |

G. Thyroid Storrm

<u>Pathophysiology</u>
- Caused by an **acute event**

<u>Patient</u>
- History of thyrotoxicosis

<u>Presentation</u>
- Tachycardia, hyperpyrexia, agitation, anxiety

<u>Physical Exam</u>
- **Goiter, lid lag**, hand tremor, and warm, moist skin

<u>Diagnostic Studies</u>
- **Low** TSH and **high** free T4 or T3

<u>Management</u>
1. Beta blocker (propranolol)
2. Thionamide (propylthiouracil or methimazole)
3. Iodine solution
4. Glucocorticoids

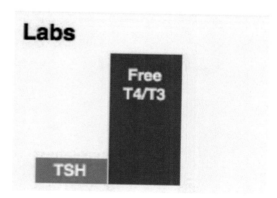

Labs

Hyperthyroid state + Acute event

Clinical

- Tachycardia (HR > 140)
- Heart failure
- Hypotension
- Dysrhythmia

- Hyperpyrexia
- Agitation
- Psychosis, stupor
- Coma

Treatment
1. Beta-blockers (Propranolol)
2. Thionamides (Propylithiouracil)
3. Iodine (Given after thionamide)
4. Glucocorticoid (Hydrocortisone)
5. Bile acid sequestrants (Cholestyramine)

Risk Factors (Acute Event)
- Surgery
- Trauma
- Infection
- Acute iodine load
- Parturition

Abbreviations

BB	Beta Blocker		**ESR**	Erythrocyte Sedimentation Rate
CCB	Calcium Channel Blocker		**ASAP**	As Soon As Possible
HTN	Hypertension		**CRP**	C-Reactive Protein
BP	Blood Pressure		**DVT**	Deep Vein Thrombosis
HR	Heart Rate		**NSAID**	Non-Steroidal Antiinflammatory
ACE	Angiotensin-Converting Enzyme		**HPV**	Human Papillomavirus
ACEI	Angiotensin-Converting Enzyme Inhibitor		**STI**	Sexually Transmitted Infection
ARB	Angiotensin II Receptor Blocker		**HSV**	Herpes Simplex Virus
CKD	Chronic Kidney Disease		**PCR**	Polymerase Chain Reaction
MI	Myocardial Infarction		**HIV**	Human Immunodeficiency Virus
HDL	High-Density Lipoprotein		**AIDS**	Acquired Immunodeficiency Syndrome
LDL	Low-Density Lipoprotein		**HHV**	Human Herpesvirus
ECG	Electrocardiogram		**CD4**	Cluster Of Differentiation 4
JVD	Jugular Venous Distension		**KOH**	Potassium Hydroxide
HTN	Hypertension		**URI**	Upper Respiratory Infection
CHF	Congestive Heart Failure		**CN**	Cranial Nerve
EF	Ejection Fraction		**TM**	Tympanic Membrane
LLSB	Lower Left Sternal Border		**HCTZ**	Hydrochlorothiazide
RUQ	Right Upper Quadrant		**Ig**	Immunoglobulin
CT	Computerized Tomography		**IM**	Intramuscular
AAA	Abdominal Aortic Aneurysm		**I&D**	Incision And Drainage
CTA	Computerized Tomography Angiography		**PCN**	Penicillin
MRA	Magnetic Resonance Angiography		**HIDA**	Hepatic Iminodiacetic Acid
MRI	Magnetic Resonance Imaging		**AMS**	Altered Mental Status
AVM	Arteriovenous Malformation		**ASCA**	Antibodies Against The Yeast *Saccharomyces Cerevisiae*

ANCA	Anti-Neutrophil Cytoplasmic Antibodies	**VCUG**	Voiding Cystourethrogram
p-ANCA	Perinuclear Anti-Neutrophil Cytoplasmic Antibodies	**UA**	Urinalysis
		TMP-SMX	Trimethoprim-Sulfamethoxazole
GI	Gastrointestinal	**CVA**	Costovertebral Angle
IBS	Irritable Bowel Syndrome	**CVA**	Cerebrovascular Accident
A-Fib	Atrial Fibrillation	**UVJ**	Ureterovesicular Junction
CAD	Coronary Artery Disease	**LDH**	Lactate Dehydrogenase
FAP	Familial Adenomatous Polyposis	**PT**	Prothrombin Time
CMV	Cytomegalovirus	**PTT**	Partial Thromboplastin Time
EGD	Esophagogastroduodenoscopy	**DIC**	Disseminated Intravascular Coagulation
GERD	Gastroesophageal Reflux Disease	**TIBC**	Total Iron Binding Capacity
LES	Lower Esophageal Sphincter	**EDTA**	Ethylenediaminetetraacetic Acid
PPI	Proton Pump Inhibitor	**G6PD**	Glucose-6-Phophatase
HAV	Hepatitis A Virus	**RBC**	Red Blood Cell
HBV	Hepatitis B Virus	**Hgb**	Hemoglobin
IVDA	Intravenous Drug Abuse	**HbF**	Fetal Hemoglobin
HEV	Hepatitis E Virus	**HSCT**	Hematopoietic Stem Cell Transplantation
AST	Aspartate Aminotransferase		
ALT	Alanine Aminotransferase	**GBM**	Glomerular Basement Membrane
IEA	Inferior Epigastric Artery	**WBC**	White Blood Cell
HUS	Hemolytic Uremic Syndrome	**ESRD**	End-Stage Renal Disease
IV	Intravenous	**ABG**	Arterial Blood Gas
IVF	Intravenous Fluid	**ADH**	Antidiuretic Hormone
CA	Carbohydrate Antigen	**DI**	Diabetes Insipidus
NGT	Nasogastric Tube	**CSF**	Cerebrospinal Fluid
		TB	Tuberculosis

Abbreviations

AFB	Acid-Fast Bacilli		**TLC**	Total Lung Capacity
PPD	Purified Protein Derivative		**FEV**	Forced Expiratory Volume
VDRL	Venereal Disease Research Laboratory		**FVC**	Forced Vital Capacity
RPR	Rapid Plasma Reagin		**LFT**	Liver Function Tests
DNA	Deoxyribonucleic Acid		**PA**	Pulmonary Arterial
PIP	Proximal Interphalangeal Joints		**PID**	Pelvic Inflammatory Disease
DIP	Distal Interphalangeal Joints		**IUD**	Intrauterine Device
PMN	Polumorphonuclear Neutrophils		**IVF**	In Vitro Fertilization
AP	Anteroposterior		**FHR**	Fetal Heart Rate
MTP	Metatarsophalangeal Joint		**TSH**	Thyroid Stimulating Hormone
RF	Rheumatoid Factor		**FSH**	Follicle Stimulating Hormone
CK	Creatine Kinase		**LH**	Luteinizing Hormone
EMG	Electromyography		**OCP**	Oral Contraceptive Pill
MCP	Metacarpophalangeal Joint		**USPSTF**	U.S. Preventive Services Task Force
CCP	Cyclic Citrullinated Peptide		**TAH**	Total Abdominal Hysterectomy
DMARD	Disease-Modifying Antirheumatic Drugs		**BSO**	Bilateral Salpingo Oophorectomy
HLA	Human Leukocyte Antigen		**LMP**	Last Menstrual Period
ROM	Range Of Motion		**PAPP-A**	Pregancy-Associated Plasma Protein A
SI	Sacroiliac		**NST**	Nonstress Test
TCA	Tricyclic Antidepressant		**SOB**	Shortness of Breath
ICP	Intracranial Pressure		**CBT**	Cognitive Behavioral Therapy
NMDA	N-Methyl-D-Aspartate			
EEG	Electroencephalogram			

Made in the USA
Middletown, DE
02 April 2021